Literacy Skills for
PAPUA NEW GUINEA

T0363270

Improve your
SPELLING
SKILLS

Susan Baing

OXFORD

OXFORD
UNIVERSITY PRESS
AUSTRALIA & NEW ZEALAND

253 Normanby Road, South Melbourne, Victoria 3205, Australia

Oxford University Press is a department of the University of Oxford.
It furthers the University's objective of excellence in research,
scholarship, and education by publishing worldwide in

Oxford New York

Auckland Cape Town Dar es Salaam Hong Kong Karachi
Kuala Lumpur Madrid Melbourne Mexico City Nairobi
New Delhi Shanghai Taipei Toronto

With offices in

Argentina Austria Brazil Chile Czech Republic France Greece
Guatemala Hungary Italy Japan Poland Portugal Singapore
South Korea Switzerland Thailand Turkey Ukraine Vietnam

OXFORD is a trademark of Oxford University Press
in the UK and in certain other countries

ISBN 978 0 19 551587 9.

Edited by Kate Deutrom and Paige Amor
Text and cover designed by Aileen Taylor
Illustrated by Melissa Webb
Typeset by Promptset Pty Ltd
Printed in Australia by Ligare Pty Ltd.

Contents

Overview—Improve Your Spelling Skills

Please use your Oxford University Press Dictionary when required.
Answer all questions in your exercise book.

To the student

This book has two parts. In the first part you will learn some of the rules of spelling that will help you spell words correctly.

Keep an exercise book where you can write the new words you learn. Then when you read something you can add any words that you find. For example, there are many words that have *ie* or *ei* in them. Write the *ie* and *ei* words you learn in your exercise book on one page, and then add any other *ie* or *ei* words that you find.

In the second part of the book you will find the spelling of some word groups. These word groups will help you learn and spell new words. Keep a separate page in your exercise book for the different word groups. As you read you can write more words on these pages.

Always try to use any new words you learn. Use the new words when you are talking to your teacher or your friends. Use the new words when you write stories, poems or letters.

To the teacher

This book aims to teach some of the rules of spelling and to increase your students' vocabulary.

Give your students some writing tasks that will help them use the new words. For example, 'Unit 21 Word groups—words about agriculture' has an exercise that asks students to write a story about the agriculture in their province (Activity D), but there are many other ways you can get students to use the words.

Encourage students to add word groups and words with similar spellings to their lists by having class competitions and making displays.

Getting spelling help from the dictionary

The words in a dictionary are always arranged in alphabetical order:

a b c d e f g h i j k l m n o p q r s t u v w x y z.

Take notice of the first letter of a word. The first letter of the word decides the order. You would look in the front of the dictionary to find *accept* and the back of the dictionary for *zinc*. Sometimes you need to go to the second or third letter to find the word.

Activity A

Arrange these lists of words in alphabetical order.

Lae, Port Moresby, Mendi, Aitape, Wewak
mango, pawpaw, pineapple, soursop, passionfruit
rust, run, ruthless, rumble, ruler
mend, meat, medium, mean, meek
depth, depend, deport, depict, deplore
pint, pin, pineapple, pincer, pink

Activity B

Complete each row by adding words of your own. The row must be in alphabetical order from left to right, like the first row.

apron	attack	catfish	door	draw	find	gate
dance		fresh		grab		jump
bray		bring		broad		brute
	sail		saw		sermon	
	fuel		fund		furry	
indeed		Indian		indoor		industry

Activity C

Some words are hard to find in the dictionary. To help you find words, try writing the word the way its sounds and look for the correct spelling.

Here are some words that are very hard to find if you don't know how to spell them. Find them in your dictionary and practise spelling them:

aisle, ceiling, fauna, pneumonia, psalm, wharf.

Activity D

A syllable is a part of a word that has a separate sound when you say it. Syllables are important in spelling because they form words.

A word can have just one syllable: *pig, run*, or it can have more syllables. Crocodile has three syllables: *croc o dile*. Say these words out loud to hear how many syllables they have:

dangerous >> dan ger ous
museum >>mu se um
adventure >> ad ven ture

Now try these:

pencil	envelope
bed	food
school	impossible
raindrop	ant

Hold a class competition to find as many three and four syllable words as you can.

2

Common letter patterns in words

The English language has some common letter patterns. Look out for these patterns. They can help you with spelling.

1. Some consonant sounds that start a word, such as *l* or *r*, are followed by a vowel: *leaf, reef*

2. Other consonant sounds, such as *b* or *f,* can be followed by another consonant: *break, flower.*

3. Not many words have more than three consonants together. Here are some: *thought, fetch, watch.*

4. Some pairs of vowels go together: *ai, ea, ee, oa, oi, ou.*

5. Not many words have more than two vowels together. Here are some: *beauty, furious, curious.*

6. A *kw* sound at the beginning of a word is usually spelled *qu: quiet, quick.*

7. A *shon* sound at the end of a word is usually spelled *ion: nation, relation.*

8. An *f* sound can be spelt *ph* or *gh: phone, tough* (*gh* can have other sounds too, so be careful).

9. Some common groups of letters are: *ation, able, ible, ious, eigh, ough.*

Activity A

1   Use your dictionary and look at some words that begin with *l* or *r*. What letters come next in the words?

2   Find and write ten examples for each of these word beginnings:

la*mp*	le	li	lo	lu
ra	re	ri	ro	ru

Find and write ten examples of words that begin with each of the two consonants:

black	gr	sn
br	kn	sp
ch	pl	sq
cl	pr	st
cr	sc	sw
dr	sh	th
fl	sk	tr
fr	sl	wh

Activity C

Find and write ten words that have each of these vowels together:

ai >> rain	oa
ea	oi
ee	ou

Activity D

Find and write ten words that begin with *qu*: *quaint*

Activity E

Find and write ten words that end with *ion*: *potion*

Activity F

Find and write ten words with *ph* or *gh* that sounds like *f*: *tough*

Word building patterns— making plurals

Common word building patterns can help you with spelling.

There are some rules to do with making nouns plural that you can learn and use.

Activity A

Many nouns add *s* to make the plural. Make these words plural by adding *s*. Write the words:

bridge >> bridges
book, desk, gate, bicycle, truck, car, hill, piano, house, cat, radio, bag, tree, airfield, bean, conclusion, filter, temperature, sauce, quarter, recipe, crumb, puzzle.

Activity B

Many nouns that end in *ch, o, sh, s, z, and x* add *es* to make the plural. Make these words plural by adding *es*. Write the words:

church >> churches
potato, tomato, wish, pass, buzz, mix, box, brush, fox, glass, watch, gas, glass, class, process, hero, echo, volcano, mango, arch, search.

Activity C

Nouns that end in a *vowel + y*, such as *ay or ey*, keep the *y* and add *s*. Make these words plural by adding *s*. Write the words:

valley >> valleys
key, bay, alley, chimney, boy, play, holiday,
stingray, way, toy, tray.

Activity D

Nouns that end in a *consonant + y*, such as *by or ly*, change the *y* to *i* and add *es*. Make these words plural by changing the *y* to *i* and adding *es*. Write the words:

lolly >> lollies
baby, lady, fly, army, city, berry, factory, diary,
country, party, story, enemy, apology, variety,
century, salary, observatory, paddy, pastry,
family, university.

Activity E

Some nouns that end in *f* or *fe* change the *f* to *v* and add *s* or *es*, such as *wife/wives*. Use your dictionary and write two lists:

wife, shelf, life, roof, belief, loaf, leaf, sheaf,
reef, wolf, thief, half, scarf, calf, chief.

Words that end in *f* or *fe* that add *s*	Words that end in *f* or *fe* that change *f* to *v* and add *s* or *es*
belief/beliefs	wife/wives

Word building patterns— prefixes and suffixes

> You can make new words by adding letters to the start of words (prefixes) and to the end of words (suffixes). For example: you add *un* (prefix) to happy to make unhappy, or add *ness* (suffix) to happy to make happiness. Note that sometimes you need to make changes in spelling.

Activity A

Underline the prefixes and suffixes in these words: *hairy*

submarine, thoughtless, untangle, friendship.

Activity B

Make new words by adding a prefix. Choose a prefix from the left column for each word and write the new word: *predict*

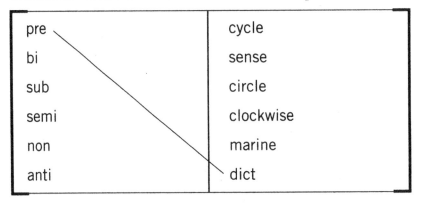

pre	cycle
bi	sense
sub	circle
semi	clockwise
non	marine
anti	dict

Activity C

Write the words you have made in these sentences. The first letter has been put in for you:

1   The crazy person was talking **n**_____.

2 The boy rode his **b**_____ to school.

3 We were told to go in an **a**_____ direction around the oval.

4 Giri drew a **s**_____ for his maths exercise.

5 The **s**_____ travelled under the ocean from Madang to Wewak.

6 We cannot truly **p**_____ when an earthquake will happen.

Activity D

Make a new word by adding a suffix. Choose a suffix from the right column and write the new word. Use your dictionary if you think the spelling needs to be changed: *childish*

child	ful
wonder	ish
care	y
motor	less
wood	en
breeze	ist

Activity E

Add suffixes to the words in brackets below to complete the sentences. Use the above list of suffixes to help you.

1 The classroom looked very _____ (cheer) with the walls brightly painted.

2 I felt _____ (fool) when I dropped my book.

3 The water was too _____ (salt) to drink.

4 The _____ (art) drew the group of children.

5 The sun looked _____ (gold) in the sky.

6 The surprise made the teacher _____ (speech).

9

Unit 4

Unit 5

Word building patterns—double consonant words

There are some rules to help you spell words with double consonants.

Activity A

A short vowel sound is usually followed by a double consonant. Say these words out loud and hear the short vowel sound: *horror*, *button*, *occur*.

Look in your dictionary and write another ten words that have double consonants.

Activity B

You use the same rule when you put endings on some words. The vowel in *hop* is a short sound, so you double the final consonant and make *hopping* and *hopped*.

Add *ing* and *ed* to these words and write the words. Say the words out loud to help you:

chop, clap, grab, step, rob, stop, sob, rip, tug, wag.

Activity C

When the vowel has a long sound, you do not double the consonant. The vowel in *hope* is a long sound, so the consonant is not doubled when you make *hoping* and *hoped*.

Add *ing* and *ed* to these words and write the words. Say the words out loud to help you:

gate, bake, moan, mind, seem, stripe, scrape, shelter, trick.

Unit  6

Silent letters

Some words are spelt with letters that you do not sound out loud. These words have *silent letters*.

Activity A

Say these words out loud. The letters in **bold** are silent. Your dictionary can help you say these words.

clim**b**	num**b**	s**c**issors	hym**n**
dou**b**t	forei**g**n	de**b**t	**g**host
knife	**k**nowledge	com**b**	**h**asten
guard	**k**nock	dum**b**	colum**n**

Activity B

Find words from the list in Activity A with these meanings. Write the word starting with the letter:

a song sung in Church	<u>hymn</u>
a tool to cut food with	k_____
a person who protects something	g_____
to hurry	h_____
to have no sense of feeling	n_____
a tool for making hair look tidy	c_____
something you owe	d_____
to make a tapping sound	k_____
a vertical part or division of a page	c_____

How to spell *ie* and *ei* words

There are three rules that can help you spell *ie* or *ei* words. You will need to say the words out loud.

1 Use *ie* when the vowel sound is *ee*: thief, piece, niece.
2 Use *ei* after *c*: receive, deceive.
3 Use *ei* when the vowel sounds is not *ee*: weight, height.

Activity A

Here are some words with *ie* or *ei* in them. Underline the *ie* or *ei* letters:

receive	thief	deceit	grief
believe	foreign	chief	neither
neighbour	deceive	friend	either
priest	freight	protein	hygiene
receipt	science	ceiling	diet

Activity B

Write the words from Activity A in two lists. Put the *ei* words on one list and the *ie* words on the other list. Leave a space to add any other *ie* or *ei* words you find when you are reading.

Activity C

Find words from Activity A with these meanings. Write the word next to the meaning. Use the first letter to help you:

1 a person living nearby: **n**_____

2 someone who steals: **t**_____

3 one of the three food groups: **p**_____

4 keeping things clean: **h**_____

5 to make someone believe something that is not true:
     d_____

6 the roof inside a house: **c**_____

7 to think that something is true: **b**_____

Write these sentences and put words from the list in Activity A in the spaces. Check in your dictionary if you are not sure of the meaning of any word:

1 To keep healthy, you must eat the right food. A good <u>diet</u> will have some <u>protein</u> in it.

2 It is not a good idea to practice **d**_____. Your friends will stop believing what you say.

3 My favourite subject at school is **s**_____ .

4 The **p**_____ at my Church is very friendly.

5 My mother is not here. She is **e**_____ in the garden, or at the river.

6 I only eat kaukau or rice. I like **n**_____ taro or yam.

7 When my grandfather died, I felt a lot of **g**_____ .

8 The boy hoped to **r**_____ a letter from his **penf**_____.

9 Sir Michael Somare is known as the **c**_____ because he is a well-known leader.

10 The shopkeeper gave me a **r**_____ when I bought some new shoes.

11 The **f**_____ was loaded onto the ship to go to Lae.

12 One day I would like to learn a **f**_____ language, such as French or German.

Write your own sentences using each word from the list.

Unit  8

Words that end in *or*, *ar* and *er*

Many words end in *or*, *ar* and *er*. Words to do with people often end in *er*: *lawyer*.

calculator	burglar	saucer
refrigerator	grammar	propeller
radiator	doctor	daughter
councillor	collar	minister
ancestor	passenger	laughter
popular	shoulder	computer

Activity A

Write the sentences with words from the list:

1 Tau pulled at the **c**_____ of his shirt.

2 Sigi used a **c**_____ to do his maths.

3 The **p**_____ on the bus did not want to pay the driver.

4 My **a**_____ was a great warrior in the days before Europeans came to this country.

5 Gabi's mother serves as a **c**_____ in the Local Government.

6 Joshua's **s**_____ was hurt in the football game.

7 Her mother put the tea in a cup with a **s**_____.

8 A **r**_____ helps you keep food fresh in hot weather.

9 The sound of l_____ makes you feel good.

10 The **m**_____ at our Church is preparing us to go on a bible camp.

Activity B

Write *or*, *ar*, or *er* on the end of these words. Check your dictionary to see if you have spelt them correctly:

pray _ _	lay _ _
numb _ _	regul _ _
wheth _ _	eith _ _
neith _ _	sciss _ _ s
terr _ _	simil _ _
recov _ _	consid _ _

Activity C

Who are these people? Find the words in your dictionary and write them. Make sure you have the right ending on the word. Here are two examples:

A person who *burgles* is a *burglar*.
A person who practises *law* is a *lawyer*.

1 A person who farms is a _____.

2 A person who paints is a _____.

3 A person who begs is a _____.

4 A person who reports is a _____.

5 A person who invents is an _____.

6 A student who boards is a board _____.

7 A person who acts is an _____.

8 A person who writes is a _____.

9 A person who teaches is a _____.

10 A person who bakes is a _____.

Unit 9

sh sound words

Some words that have *sh* sounds in them are not spelt with *sh*. These words can be spelled with *ial* or *ion*.

Activity A

Here are some words that are spelt in this way. Say them aloud and hear the *sh* sound. Now underline the letters with the *sh* sound.

educat<u>ion</u>	attention	torrential	nation
imagination	organisation	artificial	initial
congratulations	confidential	distinction	special

Add some more words when you find them in your reading or use them in your writing.

Activity B

Write the rest of the word in the spaces, then write the sentences:

1 The torrent_____ rain fell and caused a flood in the river.

2 You need to pay attent_____ in the class if you want to learn easily.

3 My mother wants me to get a good educat_____ , so I am studying hard.

4 The man got a medal because he had served his country with distinct_____ .

5 The children who lost their legs and arms in the Aitape tidal wave have got artific_____ limbs.

6 When I write stories I like to use my imagina_____ .

7 Our nat_____ has four main regions.

8 The doctor asked me what my init_____ was so that he could write it on my card.

9 The letter addressed to my mother had confident_____ written on the envelope, so I did not open it.

10 My mother cooked a spec_____ meal for my birthday.

11 The teacher said the senior students were responsible for the organisat_____ of the sports day.

12 When our team won, we said congratulat_____ to them.

Activity C

Write the sentences with words from the list in Activity A:

1 The story my friend told me was <u>confidential</u>, so I did not tell anyone else.

2 The council asked our Church Youth Group to help with the **o**_____ of the cultural show.

3 My **e** _____ will be useful when I want to start my own business in the village.

4 The **i**_____s ENB mean East New Britain.

5 The flower was made of plastic and looked very **a**_____ .

6 When you drive you have to pay **a**_____ to the other drivers on the road.

7 The artist had used a lot of **i**_____ to paint a picture of the face of the man at the Goroka Show.

8 The rain during the wet season can be **t**_____ .

Activity D

Now you write sentences using the words.

Words that end in *gh*, *th* and *ght*

Many words end in the letters *gh*, *th* and *ght*.

light	length	taught	rough
freight	breadth	thorough	cough
weight	depth	although	plough
height	through	tough	dough
straight	thought	enough	drought

Activity A

Underline the *gh*, *th* and *ght* letters in the words on the list.

Activity B

Underline the *ou+gh* words in these sentences (not all of the words are on the list):

1 We appreciate your <u>thoughtfulness</u> in writing the thankyou letter.

2 The police were told to search the house thoroughly.

3 He gave the house a thorough cleaning.

4 We had to walk through the mud to reach the road.

5 One followed by three noughts represents the number 1000.

6 The cows drank at the water trough.

7 Prices ought to come down soon.

8 The tractor pulled the plough to get the ground ready for the peanut crop.

9 The rice was bad because we did not put enough water in the saucepan.

10 Her feet had become toughened by going without shoes all her life.

Match these sentence halves and write the sentence:

1 The freight was moved	... was too weak for me to use for reading.
2 The rough play	... to Mt Hagen by truck.
3 Although I hastened,	... before planting the crop
4 She taught me	... near the island is not known.
5 The light bulb	... of the football field.
6 We measured the breadth	... job of weeding the garden.
7 You must plough the ground	... spoilt the game.
8 The depth of the ocean	... my sister's bad cough.
9 The class made a thorough	... at my Primary School.
10 The doctor treated	... I couldn't catch her.

Write adjectives from the list to describe these words:

r_____ skin
t_____ question
s_____ line
t_____ ful person
l_____ colour

Words that end in *ure*

treasure	puncture	furniture	fracture
agriculture	literature	departure	leisure
signature	pasture	pressure	culture

Activity A

Write the syllables in the correct order so they make the word:

1   (the way you write your name) ture na sig
2   (a hole in something) ture punc
3   (novels and poetry) e lit ture ra
4   (leaving) part ure de
5   (time to relax) ure leis
6   (a break in something) frac ture
7   (chairs etc) ture furn it
8   (farming) ure cult ag ri

Activity B

The mixed up letters in the brackets spell words on the list. Write the letters in the correct order, and write the sentence:

1   The boy had to stop and mend the (uercntup) on his tyre before he could ride his bike to school. (*puncture*)

2   The children played at finding the hidden (rasretue).

3   The cattle enjoyed the fresh (serutap) after the rain.

4   The driver had to check the (sreresup) of the tractor tyres before he did the ploughing.

5   We put on a show to let people see the traditional clothes which are part of our (lurtuce).

Words that end in *ue*

tongue	catalogue	vague
fatigue	avenue	morgue
plague	clue	

Activity A

Find out how to spell the *ue* word by breaking the code. Write the sentences with the correctly spelt words:

1 – a	7 – g	12 – l	17 – q	22 – v
2 – b	8 – h	13 – m	18 – r	23 – w
3 – c	9 – i	14 – n	19 – s	24 – x
4 – d	10 – j	15 – o	20 – t	25 – y
5 – e	11 – k	16 – p	21 – u	26 – z
6 – f				

1 Serah carefully licked the ice cream with her (20 15 14 7 21 5). (*tongue*)

2 A very large numbers of locusts is sometimes called a (16 12 1 7 21 5).

3 The runner felt (6 1 20 9 7 21 5) after the long race down the (1 22 5 14 21 5).

4 I help the librarian to (3 1 20 1 12 15 7 21 5) the new books.

5 The teacher gave me a (3 12 21 5) to help me answer the question about the (13 15 18 7 21 5).

6 The morning mist made the trees on the mountain look like (22 1 7 21 5) shapes.

Words with *qu*

In Unit 2 you found ten words that begin with *qu*. Are your words on this list? *Qu* is found in the middle of words too. In English words *q* is followed by *u*.

questions	squash	frequent	quick
square	mosquito	quilt	quiet
quarry	equator	quiz	quite

Activity A

Underline *qu* in the words on the list.

Activity B

Complete these sentences with words from the list above. Underline one *qu* word in the sentence and put another *qu* word in the space:

1 I tried to squash the _____ that was buzzing near my ear.

2 The teacher asked twenty _____ in the quiz.

3 We were told to move quickly and _____ly to the library.

4 The truck went frequently to the _____ for loads of stone.

5 The table was not quite _____ so the student had to make it again.

6 Papua New Guinea is located _____ near the equator.

Here are some more qu words. Check your dictionary to find out what they are (the *q* section of the dictionary is very short). Write the words and their meanings:

1 *qu* _____ a constructed place where boats can load and unload

2 *qu* _____ a line of waiting people or cars

3 *qu* _____ four people playing or singing together

4 *qu* _____ to have an argument

5 *qu* _____ to repeat someone else's words in speech or writing

6 *qu* _____ a small game bird

7 *qu* _____ one of four equal parts

Match the meanings and the words. Check your answer in the dictionary and write the words and their meanings:

squabble	a small group of people who work or play together
squad	a quarrel which is not very important
squall	a small noise like a cry such a mouse would make, or a door that needs oiling
squat	
	a small tree animal that lives in the USA and Europe
squeak	
	an animal that lives in the sea
squirrel	a sudden strong wind
squid	to sit on your heels

Write a story using as many *qu* words as you can.

Words that end in *ent* and *ant*

ent and *ant* are often found at the end of words.

relevant	important	convenient	efficient
abundant	fragrant	permanent	confident
reluctant	pleasant	obedient	frequent
elegant	distant	dependent	violent
immigrant	ignorant	incident	different
significant	inhabitant	deficient	continent

Activity A

1 Write two words from the list beginning with *c* and ending in *ent*.

2 Write two words beginning in *d* and ending in *ent*.

3 Write two words beginning in *i* and ending in *ant*.

4 Write two words beginning in *r* and ending in *ant*.

5 Write two words beginning in *e* and ending in *ent* and *ant*.

6 Write two words beginning in *f* and ending in *ent* and *ant*.

7 Write two words beginning in *p* and ending in *ent* and *ant*.

Activity B

Write the sentence with the rest of the word in the spaces:

1 The story we read in class was relev_____ to our lesson about volcanoes.

2 Birds that were abund_____ in the past are rare now.

3 The girl was reluct_____ to lend her library book.

4 The immigr_____ decided to become a citizen of his new country.

5 It is import_____ to know when the rainy season is, so you can plant the right crops.

6 When I leave school, I want to visit all the dist_____ parts of Papua New Guinea.

7 You should not be ignor_____ of the school rules.

8 The store was conveni_____ly located near the road.

9 My dog is very obedi_____.

10 In 1975 our country became independ_____ .

11 The plough is an effici_____ way to prepare soil for farming.

12 Samuel was confid_____ he would be in the team.

13 Boxing is a viol_____ sport.

14 We reported the incid_____ of theft to the headmaster.

Activity C

Match the words from the list in the left column, with a word from the right column, that has a similar meaning. Check the words in your dictionary:

elegant	perfumed
significant	unlike
fragrant	lacking
pleasant	important
inhabitant	smart
permanent	citizen
different	often
deficient	everlasting
frequent	land-mass
continent	nice

Words that end in *ible* and *able*

Words that describe things often end in *ible* and *able*.

suitable	reliable	visible
available	valuable	accessible
irritable	changeable	terrible
reasonable	admirable	convertible
dependable	agreeable	permissible
miserable	comfortable	responsible
noticeable		

Activity A

Underline the *ible* and *able* endings in the words in the list above.

Activity B

Write words from the list that mean:

1 able to be noticed
2 able to change
3 able to be admired
4 able to be depended on
5 able to be relied on
6 able to be reasoned with
7 able to get easily irritated
8 able to take responsibility

9 able to be seen

10 able to be accessed (reached)

11 able to be converted

12 able to be permitted (allowed)

Activity C

Match these sentence halves and write the sentence:

1 The librarian is responsible for	... who are reliable to help her.
2 The librarian needs students	... through the mist.
3 The new boat travelling between Lae and Madang	... looking after the library.
4 The mountains were visible	... to diesel fuel.
5 The engine is convertible	... is very comfortable.

Activity D

Check your dictionary to make sure you know the meanings of these words, then write them so that they describe the word that follows: _noticeable_ scar

agreeable, valuable, available, miserable, terrible, suitable, accessible, changeable

1 _____ person

2 _____ clothes

3 _____ weather

4 _____ accident

5 _____ watch

6 _____ rainy day

7 _____ airstrip

8 _____ ticket

16

Words that end in *ous*

> Words that describe things often end in *ous*.

glorious	unconscious	generous	strenuous
studious	suspicious	mountainous	virtuous
contagious	delicious	marvellous	continuous
spacious	religious	ridiculous	courteous
vicious	infectious	mischievous	courageous

Activity A

Write words from the list above that have similar meanings to these words. Use your dictionary to check:

violent **v**_____   silly **r**_____

roomy **s**_____   uninterrupted **c**_____

brave **c**_____   polite **c**_____

cheeky **m**_____   hilly **m**_____

amazing **m**_____   good **v**_____

Activity B

Write adjectives from the list above that go with these words:

s_____ exercise   **c**_____ rain

d_____ food   **v**_____ nun

s_____ room   **i**_____ disease

v_____ dog   **c**_____ soldier

s_____ student   **g**_____ donation

g_____ sunrise   **m**_____ land

Activity C

Write the sentences with words from the list:

1 The building was so **m**_____ that people came from overseas to see it.

2 I was very **s**_____ of the way the boys were acting.

3 The sunset was a **g**_____ red and orange.

4 If you are **s**_____ and always do your homework, the teacher will be pleased with you.

5 **I**_____ and **c**_____ are two ways to describe diseases that can spread from person to person.

6 The punch knocked the boxer **u**_____ .

7 The teacher thought the student's mistake was **r**_____ .

8 I am really tired of the **c**_____ problems with power supply.

9 The food was so **d**_____ that every bit was eaten.

Activity D

You can use some words from the list below to describe things you like and to describe things you don't like. Write two lists of these words:

generous, vicious, suspicious, contagious, spacious, infectious, courteous, courageous, mischievous

To describe things I like	To describe things I don't like
generous	vicious

Words that get mixed up

Some words look or sound nearly the same. You can sometimes get these words mixed up.

affect/effect	choose/chose	its/it's
accept/except	bought/brought	your/you're
quiet/quite	to/too	practice/practise
of/off	past/passed	advice/advise
loose/lose	their/they're	lightening/lightning

Activity A

Read the sentences then decide which word is the right one for the sentence. Write the sentence with the right word.

Example:

You're/Your These words sound the same but they have different meanings.

You're/Your a student at this school.

You're/Your class is studying science.

You're a student at this school. (*You're* means *you are*.)

Your class is studying science. (*Your* is the class that you belong to.)

1 The strong wind will *affect/effect* many villages along the coast. One *affect/effect* of the strong wind will be rough seas.

2 The teacher will not *accept/except* late homework, *accept/except* if you are sick.

3 If you want to see the cassowary, stand *quiet/quite* still and be very *quiet/quite*.

4 You should take *of/off* your football boots when you come in the door *of/off* the classroom.

5 The button on your shirt is too *loose/lose* and it will fall off. You will *loose/lose* that button on your shirt.

6 When I was asked to *choose/chose* a new dress, I *choose/chose* a red dress.

7 My friend *bought/brought* me an ice cream. It was a hot day and by the time she *bought/brought* the ice cream to me, it was melted.

8 I would like to go *to/too* Lae *to/too*, as well as Madang.

9 In the *past/passed* we dressed in traditional costumes. Some of the traditions have been *past/passed* on to the present generation.

10 Today is *their/they're* holiday, so *their/they're* going to hunt for wild pig.

11 That's my dog. The car hit *its/it's* leg. *Its/It's* been hurt.

12 It's *your/you're* turn next. Are you sure *your/you're* ready?

13 I go to basketball *practice/practise* two days a week. At home I also *practice/practise* throwing goals.

14 My teacher wanted to *advice/advise* me to work harder because my marks were not good. Her *advice/advise* was to spend more time learning new words.

15 The day began with thunder and *lightening/lightning*. After the storm passed, we saw that the sky was *lightening/lightning* over the valley and the sun was coming out.

Unit 17

Unit 18

Word groups—happy words

glad	excellent	cheerful	pleased
lucky	excitement	joyful	miracle
convenient	familiar	independence	patience
courtesy	contented	laugh	sincere
easier	favourite	loveliest	successful

Activity A

Write words from the list with these meanings. Check your answers with the meanings in your dictionary:

1 A word to describe a feeling you have when things go well. **g**_____

2 A word to describe a feeling being relaxed and happy. **c**_____

3 A word for an event that is wonderful, magical and unexpected. **m**_____

4 A word to describe what you do when you feel happy. **l**_____

5 A word for a feeling you have while waiting for something good to happen. **e**_____

6 Another word for truly felt or meant. **s**_____

7 A word for a feeling you hope someone will have for you, when you are having trouble learning. **p**_____

8 A word to describe something that you always prefer. **f**_____

9 Another word for polite manners. **c**_____

10 A word for the most lovely. **l**_____

Match these words with a phrase that has a similar meaning. Write the words and the meanings:

lucky	less difficult
convenient	doing very well at something
independent	a feeling of happiness
pleased	the very best of something
easier	fortunate, having good luck
familiar	not having to depend on something
favourite	easy to use
cheerful	the most lovely
joyful	something well known to you
loveliest	full of joy
successful	the one you like best
excellent	happy and satisfied

Use the words in *italics* to describe the words from the box. There is more than one answer for some words:

lucky, easier, favourite, excellent,
familiar, sincere, convenient

exam	ticket	feeling	shirt
marks	person	journey	guess
question	time	food	essay

Write a story about a happy time. Use as many words from the list as you can. Use other happy words that you know too.

Word groups—words about our world

country	desert	island	drought
population	altitude	longitude	monsoon
equator	latitude	tropical	ocean
earth	continent	climate	gulf

Activity A

Write pair words from these words:

1	country	large area of land
2	altitude	line on a map
3	equator	height
4	continent	hot
5	tropical	nation

1	climate	flood
2	drought	weather
3	monsoon	desert
4	latitude	Pacific
5	ocean	location

Activity B

Write the sentences with words from the list above:

1 The **e**_____ is the planet where we live.

2 The imaginary line around the middle of the earth is the **e**_____.

3 The lines on a map are the lines of **l**_____ and **l**_____.

4 Large areas of land are called **c**_____**s**.

5 Small areas of land in the sea, such as Fiji are **i**_____**s**.

6 The height of a mountain is its **a**_____.

7 D_____ areas do not get much rain.

8 A d_____ is a long time without rain.

9 Many tropical countries have m_____ rains.

10 The p_____ of a country is the number of people who live there.

11 The name of our c_____ is Papua New Guinea.

12 Madang, where it is hot and wet, has a tropical c_____.

Activity C

Match the people, things or animals with the place:

1 camels	continent
2 rainforest	ocean
3 heavy rain	island
4 whales and dolphins	desert
5 coconuts and reefs	tropics
6 Asia	monsoon

Activity D

Write a name for these places. Use an Atlas to help you:

a continent _____
an island _____
a desert _____
a country that has monsoons _____
an ocean _____
a gulf _____
a country, which is a neighbour _____
a country on the equator _____

Activity E

Write a sentence for each answer in Activity D.

Word groups—words about time

present	year	tomorrow	o'clock
past	calendar	yesterday	date
future	decade	earlier	week-days
memory	annual	daily	weekend
fortnight	century	anniversary	generations

Activity A

Find out how to spell the *time* words by breaking the code. Write the words. Then make up some codes of your own using time words on the list.

1–a	7–g	12–l	17–q	22–v
2–b	8–h	13–m	18–r	23–w
3–c	9–i	14–n	19–s	24–x
4–d	10–j	15–o	20–t	25–y
5–e	11–k	16–p	21–u	26–z
6–f				

1 3, 5, 14, 20, 21, 18, 25

2 4, 1, 9, 12, 25

3 5, 1, 18, 12, 9, 5, 18

4 6, 21, 20, 21, 18, 5

5 25, 5, 1, 18

Activity B

Finish these sentences with words from the list:

1 A ten-year period is a **d**_____.

2 Two weeks are called a **f**_____.

3 The time we are living in is called the **p**_____.

4 Something that happens ever year is an **a**_____ event.

5 One hundred years is called a **c**_____.

6 Parents, grandparents and children are examples of **g**_____ .

7 The day before today is called **y**_____.

8 We use a **c**_____ to find out which day of the year it is.

9 Saturday and Sunday are the days of the **w**_____.

10 When you think about the past, you use your **m**_____.

Activity C

1 The weekdays are _____.

2 Yesterday was _____ (day).

3 Tomorrow is _____.

4 This year is _____ (date).

5 The date today is _____.

6 An annual event in Papua New Guinea is _____.

7 We celebrate the anniversary of Independence on _____.

8 We start school at _____o'clock.

9 My grandfather is from a different _____.

10 We are living in the _____ century.

Activity D

Write a short story about your life using as many of the words from the list as you can.

Word groups—words about agriculture

crop	prune	cocoa	subsistence
livestock	weed	coconut	cash
cultivate	manure	coffee	export
plant	compost	tea	market
plough	irrigate	rubber	transport

Activity A

Match these sentences halves, then write the sentences:

1 When you export a crop	... you put food scraps and weeds back into the soil.
2 When you cultivate the soil	... you cut off the unwanted branches.
3 When you make compost	... you use a tractor.
	... you send it out of the country.
4 When you plough	
5 When you weed your garden	... you put animal waste on it.
6 When you prune a tree	... you get rid of the unwanted plants.
7 When you irrigate the land	... you put water on it.
	... you turn it over and make it ready for the new plants.
8 When you manure a crop	

Make and write pairs of the words:

coconut	crop
rubber	pod
cash	plantation
irrigation	berries
coffee	leaf
tea	pump
cocoa	palm

Write a word from the list in the following sentences:

1 The best time to **p** _____ peanuts is just before the rain finishes.

2 If there is not enough rain for your crop, you may need to **i**_____ the plants.

3 Chicken **m**_____ is good for growing vegetables.

4 Cattle and pigs are common **l**_____ found in Papua New Guinea.

5 You need to have a **m**_____ for your crops so that you can make some money from selling them.

6 **T**_____ to a market is a big problem in PNG.

7 Coffee trees need to be **p**_____**d** so that they produce more berries.

8 Many people in Papua New Guinea do not sell crops. They are **s**_____ farmers.

Write a short story about the agriculture in your Province.

Unit 22

Word groups—what's your job?

journalist	secretary	councillor	carpenter
reporter	wholesaler	store-keeper	pilot
referee	clerk	burglar	driver
lawyer	interpreter	librarian	engineer
technician	nurse	scientist	mechanic

Activity A

Write one word from the list for:

1 A person who breaks into houses to steal. **b** _____

2 A person who is skilful in a particular job, such as mending computers. **t** _____

3 A person who translates between languages. **i** _____

4 A person who looks after the office and makes appointments for an employer. **s** _____

5 A member of a council. **c** _____

6 A person who builds bridges and roads. **e** _____

7 A person who looks after a collection of books. **l** _____

8 A person who understands how car engines work and can fix them. **m** _____

9 A person who sells things in a store. **s** _____

10 A person who buys goods from a producer and sells them to a storekeeper. **w** _____

11 A person who works in science to find out things. **s** _____

12 A person who writes stories for the newspaper. **j** _____

13 A person who reports news for the radio or newspaper.
r _____

14 A person who makes decisions in a sporting match between two teams. r _____

15 A person who has studied the law. l _____

Activity B

Write the sentences with words from the list:

A _____ would use a whistle.
A _____ would use steering wheel.
A _____ would use hammer.
A _____ would use a bandage.
A _____ would use a till.
A _____ would use a test-tube.

Activity C

Below are activities that you might do if you chose the careers from the list. Which person from the list would do these things? Write the word in the space:

1 This is what a _____ might do: give change, help customers, and put goods on shelves.

2 This is what a _____ might do: take off, land, use a map.

3 This is what an _____ might do: listen to someone talking, change Motu into English, translate in a court.

4 This is what a _____ might do: break a window, steal a TV, take some money.

5 This is what a _____ might do: put books on shelves, stamp dates in books, help students find books.

6 This is what a _____ might do: make decisions for the council ward, work out a budget, listen to the people's needs.

Unit 23

Word groups—words about cooking

mix	quarters	mixture	recipe
peel	sauce	thicken	crumbs
grate	juice	squeeze	ingredients
simmer	refrigerate	temperature	mackerel
boil	taste	moderate	tomato

Activity A

Write words from the above list to complete the following recipe:

Savoury mackerel in tomato sauce

ING_____ :

tin of mackerel   tomatoes (tinned or fresh)
butter   limes
fresh ginger root

PREPARATION:

G_____ some cleaned ginger root and mix it with chopped fresh or tinned **t**_____. Melt some butter in a frying pan. Put in the tomatoes and ginger. The pan should not be too hot. Make sure the heat is **m**_____. Open a tin of **m**_____, and add it to the **ing**_____ in the pan. Get some limes and cut them into **q**_____. Arrange the fish on a plate and pour over the **mix**_____ from the pan. Decorate with the limes. You can **sq**_____ the lime **j**_____ on. If you have any food left over, you can **r**_____ it, because the **t**_____ gets better and you can eat it cold as well.

Activity B

Write a word from the list that means:

1 the things that go together to make up a recipe _____
2 how hot or cold something is _____
3 to keep something cold _____
4 to cook slowly _____
5 to cook quickly _____
6 tiny pieces of bread or cake _____
7 to make a sauce or soup thicker _____
8 to take the skin off fruit or vegetables _____

Activity C

Write words from the list that go with these words:

1 _____ the kaukau, please.
2 _____ the flour and water, please.
3 _____ the water for tea, please.
4 _____ the soup to see if there is enough salt, please.
5 _____ the juice from the oranges, please.
6 _____ the tapioca (cassava), please.
7 _____ the left over rice, please.
8 _____ the sauce with some flour, please.

Activity D

Do you like cooking? Write your own recipe, using as many of the words on the list as you can.

Unit 24

Word groups—words about music

rhythm	concert	audience	cassette
rhyme	stage	drums	trumpet
piano	radio	guitar	harmony
tune	melody	bass	discord
play	notes	flute	voice

Activity A

The letters in the following words from the list are in the wrong order. Put them in the right order and write the word in these sentences:

1   Another name for beat is <u>hhymtr</u>.

2   In a song, words that sound the same at the end of the line <u>emhyr</u>.

3   You need to hear the <u>ceiov</u> of the person singing on the <u>sgeat</u>.

4   In a song or piece of music there are <u>tosen</u>, which make up the <u>leydom</u> or <u>tenu</u>.

5   If the notes fit together well, you have a good sound, or <u>omynarh</u>, but if they don't you have a bad sound, or <u>cordsid</u>.

Activity B

Some of the words on the list can be made into adjectives. Follow the instructions and write the adjective you make.

Example:

melody (change the *y* to *i* and add *c*) <u>*melodic*</u>

1 melody (take away the *y* and add *i* and *ous*) _____

2 rhythm (add *ic*) _____

3 tune (add *ful*) _____

4 tune (add *less*) _____

5 harmony (take away *y* and add *ious*) _____

6 discord (add *ant*) _____

7 rhyme (take away *e* and add *ing*) _____

Activity C

Write plural words from these words. Follow the instructions:

1 Add *s* to these words: rhythm, rhyme, piano, concert, radio, audience, guitar, flute, cassette, trumpet, discord, voice.

2 Add *es* to the word: bass

3 Change the *y* to *i* and add *es*: melody, harmony

Activity D

Write the story using words from the list:

The Music Club Concert

Our music club decided to give a **c**_____.

    We have a band with some different instruments in it. There are two **g**_____s in the band. One of the guitars is a **b**_____ guitar. We also have a set of **d**_____, a **t**_____ and a **f**_____. We asked a teacher to play the **p**_____.

    We used a **c**_____ to record some **t**_____s from the **r**_____, and began to practise.

    I guess we did a good job, because the **a**_____ enjoyed the performance and asked us to put on some more **c**_____s . They said we were so good we should make a **c**_____ of the band to sell.

Unit 25

Word groups—words about sports and games

hero	athletics	challenge	oval
referee	supporter	association	boundary
unsporting	contestant	spectators	champion
player	entry	arena	draw
half-time	time-out	field	team

Activity A

Use the following letters to write words of four or five letters from the list. You can use the letters more than once in each word:

h	v	r	y	i	p
n	e	l	w	d	t
o	a	f	t	f	m

Activity B

Sort out the letters to find out what nouns from the list could go with these words. Write the words:

Example: *fair ypalre* > <u>fair player</u>

1 late   yenrt
2 popular   roeh
3 noisy   ttrsoacspe
4 soccer   ward
5 well-kept   anaer

Write words from the list that have similar meanings:

b_____ edge of the oval

t_____ side of players

c_____ competition between teams

r_____ person who keeps the rules

c_____ person who is the best player

a_____ group of teams

Match these sentence halves and write the sentences:

1. The journalist wrote	... a time-out.
2. The new team	... was a draw.
3. The spectators	... challenged the champions.
4. The referee called for	
5. Gia was a contestant in	... cheered their team loudly.
6. We sent a strong team of runners to	... the athletics competition.
7. It is unsporting to complain	... about the soccer game.
8. The contestants did not agree	... with the referee's decision.
9. The team was unhappy because the final score	... so we missed the competition.
10. Our entry was late	... the 500 metre race.
	... about losing the game.

Write a report of a game or competition you have watched, using as many words from the list as you can.

Word groups—words about cars

highway	driving test	second-hand
safety-sticker	driver	steering
windshield	spare tyre	brakes
wipers	puncture	road rules
vehicle	registration	route
license	manual gears	Public Motor Vehicle (PMV)
four-wheel drive	automatic gears	

Activity A

There are many rules about driving a car or truck. Complete these sentences using words from the list:

1 You need to have a **l**_____ before you can drive.

2 To get a license, you need to sit a **d**_____**t**_____.

3 You need to know all the **r**_____ **r**_____ before you drive a car.

4 Every car needs to have a **r**_____ sticker.

5 You must show the registration sticker on the **w**_____.

6 A car needs to have a **s**_____-**s** _____ before you can drive it on the road.

7 It is important that your **b**_____ and **s**_____ work well, or you could have an accident.

8 You need to have good windshield **w**_____ if you drive when it is raining.

9 You can choose a car, which has **a**_____ gears or **m**_____ gears.

10 Make sure your **s**_____ **t**_____ is pumped up, so you can put it on the car if you have a **p**_____.

Match these sentence halves and write the sentence:

1 A vehicle is another name	... is cheaper to buy than a new one.
2 PMVs are very busy	... how you must drive on the road.
3 If you buy a second-hand car you should	... in Port Moresby.
4 Driving without a license	... for a car, truck, bus or PMV.
5 The highway from Lae to the Highlands is called..	... will get you into trouble.
6 A second-hand car	... get the steering and brakes checked by a mechanic.
7 You need four-wheel drive	... it is hard for the driver to see the road.
8 If the windshield is cracked	... to drive on a muddy road.
9 You need to use a spare	... tyre when you have a puncture.
10 The road rules tell you	... Route 100.

Write two paragraphs about a vehicle you have been in. What was the vehicle like? Where did you go?

Word groups—words about travelling

Have you ever wanted to go travelling to another place? Here are some words you might need if your wish comes true.

passport	departure	airport	boat
visa	arrival	documents	cabin
ticket	tourism	bags	seatbelt
booking	label	counter	lifeboat
timetable	destination	wharf	trip

Activity A

Make pairs of these words and write them together:

1	booking	suitcase
2	timetable	tag
3	bag	reservation
4	passport and visa	journey
5	label	papers
6	trip	schedule

Activity B

Write one word from the above list in the spaces:

1 The place you hope to travel to **d**_____

2 The industry of travel **t**_____

3 Leaving on your journey **d**_____

4 A small room on a ship **c**_____

5 What you must use on a plane **s**_____

6 The place aircraft leave from **a**_____

7 What you would use if a ship sank **l**_____

8 A general name for the papers such as passport and visa you need to travel overseas with **d**_____

9 What you need before you get on a ship or plane **t**_____

10 What you carry your belongings in **b**_____

Activity C

Make verbs from these nouns:

1 arrival _____ to arrive

2 departure _____

3 tourism _____

4 booking _____

Activity D

Find words from the list to go in the spaces below, and write the story. Then write your own story about travel.

Last year I had a chance to go on a _____ to Sydney with my cousin. My cousin checked the _____ to see when the planes go. She made a _____ for us, and bought the _____. Because we were travelling overseas we needed to get some _____, such as a _____ and a _____. We were given some ideas about where to go in Sydney by the _____Office.

At last the day came. We were at the _____very early to catch our plane. We went up to the _____and showed the woman our _____. She gave us our boarding passes. I put my _____on the weighing machine and the woman put a _____on it, which said Sydney. I still could not believe I was going on this trip! When we got on the plane I listened to what the cabin crew said, and put on my _____. We were off to our exciting _____.

Word groups—words about thoughts

enjoy	argue	worry	dream
accept	choose	agree	forget
apologise	hope	debate	astonish
believe	condemn	worship	doubt
forgive	guess	hate	wish

Activity A

Write the correct ending for the words:

1	for		joy
2	en		ry
3	ar		ish
4	wor		ship
5	aston		gue
6	con		give
7	wor		demn
8	de		bate

Activity B

Write these sentences with words from the list:

1 You will have to **c**_____ one book or the other book.

2 My mother will **w**_____ about me if I am late.

3 I h_____ that I can start my own chicken farm.

4 The judge was ready to c_____ the murderer.

5 This amazing trick will a_____ you.

6 If you have done something wrong in the classroom, you need to a_____ to the teacher.

7 I do not know the answer, so I will g_____.

8 I h_____ snakes.

9 I did something wrong and I would like you to f___ me.

10 I b_____ that everyone can do something well.

11 It is good to f_____ about bad things in the past.

12 I a_____ that not everyone thinks the same way as me.

13 Do you a_____ with what I think?

14 I told my friend about what I d_____t last night.

15 Which Church do you go to w_____ in?

16 I always e_____ going to Church.

17 The students started to a_____ about who was to blame for the trouble.

18 I d_____d with the teacher about bride-price.

19 I d_____ that I can finish my homework on time.

20 I w_____ we didn't have to do any homework!

Activity C

Match these verbs and nouns and write them together:

Verbs		Nouns	
hate	argue	forgiveness	doubt
forgive	agree	astonishment	argument
doubt	choose	agreement	apology
astonish	apologise	choice	hatred
accept	enjoy	enjoyment	acceptance

Unit 29

Word groups—words about our senses

Here are some words you can use to describe things that you see, hear, smell, touch or taste. Use them in the exercises.

Sight	Hearing	Smell	Touch	Taste
distorted	shrill	musty	sharp	sour
blurred	squeal	putrid	prickly	savoury
scary	tuneful	aromatic	rough	succulent
beautiful	wailing	pleasant	gentle	salty
dark	sighing	floral	smooth	bitter
colourful	noisy	spicy	tepid	sweet

Activity A

What is the feel of?

sandpaper _____

pigs' skins _____

patting a cat _____

limestone rocks _____

a light wind _____

baby's bath water _____

Activity B

What is the sound of?

the whistle at half-time ____

birdsong _____

contentment _____

brakes that need oiling ___

a live band _____

a crying child _____

Activity C

What do these things look like?

myself in a trick mirror _____	a bird of paradise _____
a secret cave _____	view from a fast moving car _____
an enormous snake _____	a bright hibiscus flower ___

Activity D

What is the smell of?

something rotten _____	a garden _____
perfume _____	a closed up room _____
roasting coffee _____	ginger _____

Activity E

What is the taste of?

sugar _____	a green mango _____
sea water _____	quinine medicine _____
a juicy pawpaw _____	a meat pie _____

Activity F

Match the opposites and write them together:

1 smooth	clear	1 noisy	ugly
2 blurred	blunt	2 beautiful	quiet
3 salty	sweet	3 prickly	colourless
4 tepid	rough	4 sour	light
5 bitter	boiling	5 dark	sweet
6 sharp	sugary	6 colourful	fresh
7 shrill	tuneful	7 musty	smooth

Unit 30

Word groups—words about culture

family	tradition	lakatoi	dances
extended family	culture	kina shell	kundu drums
pig exchange	custom	feathers	funeral
bride-price	Kula	clay pots	feast
conch shell	Hiri	sago	legend

Activity A

Find the words from the list above that are within the jumbled words below:

1 b<u>lakato</u>in   *lakatoi*
2 perdancest
3 offeatherst
4 interfamilyald
5 consagose
6 perfuneralise
7 supercustomite
8 bilegendcourt
9 malfeastage
10 comboculturate

Activity B

Write a story about your culture. Use words from the list and any other words you know about culture.

Match the sentence halves, and then write the sentences:

1. Our family makes clay	… person one year after they die.
2. Our clan has a legend	
3. We exchange special bananas	… when we teach the children our language.
4. We live with our aunt, uncles	… about how the bird of paradise got its colours.
5. The lakatoi was used for the	… pigs are killed.
6. In Milne Bay shells are	… traded in the Kula ring.
7. Many things such as language and	… for bride-price
8. We have a feast for a dead	… call the members of the clan to come and meet.
9. Our clan cries for many days	… pots and trades them.
10. The conch shell was used to	… and other members of our extended family
11. A pig exchange means many	… dances are made from feathers.
12. Many headdresses that are used for	… Hiri trade.
13. We help keep our tradition	… culture from our extended families.
14. Sago was traditionally	… customs make up a clan's culture.
15. The kina shell was traded	… into the Highlands, and used for wearing.
16. We learn about	… when there is a funeral.
	… traded for clay pots.

Word groups—words about business

profit	calculator	office	account book
loss	tax	export	letter
wholesale	accounts	import	envelop
customer	buy	transport	cheque
retail	sell	bank loan	bank account

Activity A

Write the right ending for the words:

calcu	port
che	ounts
acc	lator
whole	sale
ret	ail
let	que
ex	ter

Activity B

Find a word from the list that has a similar meaning. Write the word and its meaning:

1 To send goods out of the country. **e**_____
2 To bring goods into the country. **i**_____
3 To pay money for something. **b**_____
4 To give goods in exchange for money. **s**_____

5 To move your goods from one place to a different place. **t**_____

6 The name for the extra money you get when you sell something for more than it cost you. **p**_____

7 The name for when you do not get as much money as something cost you. **l**_____

8 The name for a written instruction to a bank to pay money out of your account. **c**_____

9 A name for the records of how your money has been spent. **a**_____ **b**_____

10 What you put a letter inside. **e**_____

Activity C

Join the sentence halves and write the sentences:

1 An office is where the	... a wholesale store.
2 Money collected from taxes	... to start their business.
3 A retailer gets store goods from	... businessman does his business.
4 The retail store sells to	... make a profit.
5 A profit is when you make more	... bank account for your business.
6 You need to open a	... in an account book.
7 Some businesses need a bank loan	... is used by the government.
8 You need to write your profit and costs	... money than your costs.
9 A calculator will help you	... the customer.
10 A loss is when you do not	... keep your accounts.

Unit 32

Word groups—words about medicine

Have you ever been sick? Here are some of the words you might use.

infectious	preventable	acquired	hospital
bandage	malaria	immune	clinic
injection	malnutrition	deficiency	patient
medicine	pneumonia	syndrome	emergency
ulcer	diarrhoea	typhoid	ambulance

Activity A

Find the muddled word in the sentence. Put the letters in the right order and write the sentence.

1 You can get <u>lamaari</u> if an infected mosquito bites you (malaria).

2 You can get hidaarore if you drink water from a water supply, which is not clean.

3 If stay in the hospital, you are a tenpati.

4 If you have an accident you go to the germeenyc entrance of the hospital.

5 An cublamean is a special vehicle for carrying sick people.

6 A doctor can give you some denemiic to help you get well again.

7 The posthila is where you go to find medicine when you are sick.

8 Sometimes you need an ejiiotcnn to help your sore get better.

9 If a disease can be caught from another person, it is tifinsocue.

10 A dabagen is a strip of cloth you put on to keep flies off your sore.

Activity B

Find the word from the list to fit in the space and then write the sentence:

1 **P**_____ is a disease of the lungs.

2 A nurse can put a **b**_____ on your sore.

3 Both pneumonia and diarrhoea are **p**_____ if you take good care of you health.

4 AIDS or **A**_____ **I**_____
D_____ **S**_____ is a growing problem in Papua New Guinea.

5 Most people in rural areas do not live near to a **h**_____

6 Some villages have a **c**_____ to treat common diseases and problems.

7 Many **i**_____ diseases can be prevented if you are careful about hygiene.

8 **T**_____ is common in the Eastern Highlands.

9 If you let flies sit on a sore, it can turn into an **u**_____.

10 **M**_____ is a problem for some children.

Activity C

Write a story about the health problems in your Province. Use as many words from the list as you can.

Unit 33

Word groups—words to use for discussing ideas

Sometimes we have an argument with our friends. Sometimes we have a debate. A debate is a discussion or argument between two teams of speakers.

argument	plan	support	side
argue	think	agree	speaker
arguing	facts	opposed to	introduction
summary	opinion	opponent	conclusion

Activity A

Find words from the list that have similar meanings to the underlined words in the sentences. Write each sentence using the word from the list:

1 I like to <u>debate</u> with my friends.

2 Many people are <u>against</u> capital punishment.

3 The <u>ending</u> of the story was very sad.

4 The <u>beginning</u> told us what we would read about in the chapter.

5 The <u>main points at the end</u> reminded us of what we had read.

6 You need to have some good ideas so you can win an argument against the <u>person who is against your idea</u>.

7 I told the headmaster my <u>point of view</u> about the rules.

8 I used some <u>true ideas</u> to help make the headmaster agree with me.

9 I wanted to be the first <u>person who speaks</u> in the debate.

10 The boy was always <u>quarrelling</u> with his father.

Match these verbs and nouns and write them together:

Verbs	Nouns
argue	support
plan	plan
think	argument
support	agreement
agree	thought

Find the word from the list on page 62 to fit in the space and then write the sentence:

1   A debate is an **a**_____
    between two teams of speakers.

2   The first speaker in a debate gives an
    i_____ to her team's
    ideas for the debate.

3   The last speaker on the team makes
    a **s**_____ of the main points
    her team gave during the debate.

4   When you are **a**_____ in a debate you
    need to have some **f**_____ to help your
    argument.

5   The person who argues against you is your
    o_____.

6   You need to **s**_____ the other members of
    your team when you debate.

7   Your **s**_____ needs to **p**_____ your ideas
    carefully before the debate.

8   You need to **a**_____ about what you are going to
    say.

34

Word groups—words to use when applying for a job

apply	headmaster	advertised	application
clerk	results	certificate	supervisor
reference	interview	finished	experience
enclose	photocopy	punctual	position

Activity A

Join the two halves of the words and write them so they are spelt correctly:

applic	master
refer	view
photo	ised
head	ation
inter	copy
advert	ual
certif	tion
punct	ience
posi	ence
exper	icate

Write this letter using words from the list:

Dear Sir or Madam

I would like to **a**_____ for the position of **c**_____
that was **a**_____ in yesterday's newspaper.

I **f**_____ my Grade 8 in 2004. I **e**_____
a **ph**_____ of the **c**_____ with my
r_____.

   During my holidays I did work **e**_____
at The Department of Lands. My **s**_____ there,
Mr Hebou, will tell you about me and give you a
r_____. You can also get a **r**_____
from my school **h**_____.

   I would be happy to come for an **i**_____at any
time.

Yours faithfully

Join the words that go together:

1 school	machine	**1** finished	boss
2 enclose	headmaster	**2** supervisor	job
3 photocopy	punctual	**3** advertised	apply
4 results	inside	**4** position	completed
5 on time	marks	**5** application	newspaper

Now write your own letter, using as many words from the list as
you can.

Answers

Unit 1 Getting spelling help from the dictionary

A Aitape, Lae, Mendi, Port Moresby, Wewak
mango, passionfruit, pawpaw, pineapple, soursop
ruler, rumble, run, rust, ruthless
mean, meat, medium, meek, mend
depend, depict, deplore, deport, depth
pin, pincer, pineapple, pink, pint

D Syllables: pen/cil, bed, school, rain/drop, en/vel/ope, food,
im/poss/ib/le, ant

Unit 3 Word building patterns—making plurals

A books, desks, gates, bicycles, trucks, cars, hills, pianos,
houses, cats, radios, bags, trees, airfields, beans, conclusions,
filters, temperatures, sauces, quarters, recipes, crumbs,
puzzles

B potatoes, tomatoes, wishes, passes, buzzes, mixes, boxes,
brushes, foxes, glasses, watches, gases, glasses, classes,
processes, heroes, echoes, volcanoes, mangoes, arches,
searches

C keys, bays, alleys, chimneys, boys, plays, holidays, stingrays,
ways, toys, trays

D babies, ladies, flies, armies, cities, berries, factories, diaries,
countries, parties, stories, enemies, apologies, varieties,
centuries, salaries, observatories, paddies, pastries, families,
universities

E wives, shelves, lives, roofs, beliefs, loaves, leaves, sheaves,
reefs, wolves, thieves, halves, scarves, calves, chiefs

Unit 4 Word building patterns—prefixes and suffixes

A <u>sub</u>marine, thought<u>less</u>, <u>un</u>tangle, friend<u>ship</u>

B predict, bicycle, submarine, semicircle, nonsense,
anticlockwise

C 1. bicycle 2. **n**onsense 3. **a**nticlockwise 4. **s**emicircle
   5. **s**ubmarine 6. **p**redict

D childish, wonderful, careless, motorist, wooden, breezy

F 1. cheerful 2. I foolish 3. salty 4. artist 5. golden 6. speechless

Unit 5 Word building patterns—double consonant words

B chopping, chopped; clapping, clapped; grabbing, grabbed;
   preferring, preferred; robbing, robbed; stopping, stopped;
   sobbing, sobbed; refuelling, refuelled; ripping, ripped;
   tugging, tugged; wagging, wagged

C acting, acted; baking, baked; cooking, cooked; offering,
   offered; seeming, seemed; striping, striped; scraping, scraped;
   sheltering, sheltered; tricking, tricked

Unit 6 Silent letters

B knife, guard, hasten, numb, comb, debt, knock, column

Unit 7 How to spell *ie* and *ei* words

C 1. **n**eighbour, 2. thief, 3. **p**rotein, 4. **h**ygiene, 5. deceive,
   6. ceiling, 7. **b**elieve

D 2. **d**eceit 3. science 4. **p**riest 5. either 6. neither 7. grief.
   8. receive, penfriend 9. chief 10. receipt 11. freight
   12. foreign

Unit 8 Words that end in *or*, *ar* and *er*

A 1. collar 2. calculator 3. **p**assenger 4. ancestor 5. **c**ouncillor
   6. shoulder 7. saucer 8. **r**efrigerator 9. laughter 10. **m**inister

B prayer, layer, number, regular, whether, either, neither,
   scissors, terror, similar, recover, consider

C 1. farmer 2. painter 3. beggar 4. reporter 5. inventor
   6. boarder 7. actor 8. writer 9. teacher 10. baker

Unit 9 *sh* sound words

B 1. torrential 2. attention 3. education 4. distinction
   5. artificial 6. imagination 7. nation 8. initial 9. confidential
   10. special 11. organisation 12. congratulations

C 2. **o**rganisation 3. education 4. **i**nitials 5. **a**rtificial
   6. attention 7. **i**magination 8. **t**orrential

Unit 10 Words that end in *gh*, *th* and *ght*

B 1. thoughtfulness 2. thoroughly 3. thorough 4. through
5. noughts 6. trough 7. ought 8. plough 9. enough
10. toughened

C 1. The freight was moved to Mt Hagen by truck. 2. The
rough play spoilt the game. 3. Although I hastened, I
couldn't catch up with her. 4. She taught me at my
community school. 5. The light bulb was too weak for me to
use for reading. 6. We measured the breadth of the football
field for our maths class. 7. You must plough the ground
before the crop can be planted. 8. The depth of the ocean
near the island is not known. 9. The class made a thorough
job of weeding the garden. 10. The doctor treated my sister's
bad cough.

D rough skin, tough question, straight line, thoughtful person,
light colour

Unit 11 Words that end in *ure*

B signature, puncture, literature, departure, leisure, fracture,
furniture, agriculture

C 1. puncture 2. treasure 3. pasture 4. pressure 5. culture

Unit 12 Words that end in *ue*

A 2. plague 3. fatigue, avenue 4. catalogue 5. clue, morgue
6. vague

Unit 13 Words with *qu*

B 1. squash the mosquito 2. questions in the quiz
3. quickly and quietly 4. frequently to the quarry
5. quite square 6. quite near the equator

C 1. quay 2. queue 3. quartet 4. quarrel 5. quote 6. quail
7. quarter

D squabble—a quarrel which is not very important;
squad—a small group of people who work or play together;
squall—a sudden strong wind; squat—to sit on your heels;
squeak—a small noise like a cry such a mouse would make;
squirrel—a small tree animal that lives in America and
Europe; squid—an animal that lives in the sea

Unit 14 Words that end in *ent* and *ant*

C elegant—smart, significant—important, fragrant—perfumed, pleasant—nice, inhabitant—citizen, permanent—everlasting, different—unlike, deficient—lacking, frequent—often, continent—land-mass

Unit 15 Words that end in *ible* and *able*

B 1. noticeable 2. changeable 3. admirable 4. dependable 5. reliable 6. reasonable 7. irritable 8. responsible 9. visible 10. accessible 11. convertible 12. permissible

C 1. The librarian is responsible for looking after the library. 2. The librarian needs students who are reliable to help her. 3. The new boat travelling between Lae and Madang is very comfortable. 4. The mountains were visible through the mist. 5. The engine is convertible to diesel fuel.

D 1. agreeable person 2. suitable clothes 3. changeable weather 4. terrible accident 5. valuable watch 6. miserable rainy day 7. accessible airstrip 8. available ticket

Unit 16 Words that end in *ous*

A violent **v**icious, silly **r**idiculous, roomy **s**pacious, uninterrupted **c**ontinuous, brave **c**ourageous, polite **c**ourteous, cheeky **m**ischievous, hilly **m**ountainous, amazing **m**arvellous, good **v**irtuous

B **s**trenuous exercise, **c**ontinuous rain, **d**elicious food, **v**irtuous nun, **s**pacious room, **i**nfectious disease, vicious dog, **c**ourageous soldier, **s**tudious student, **g**enerous donation, **g**lorious sunrise, **m**ountainous land

C 1. **m**arvellous 2. suspicious 3. **g**lorious 4. **s**tudious 5. Infectious and **c**ontagious 6. **u**nconscious 7. **r**idiculous. 8. **c**ontinuous 9. **d**elicious

D Like—generous, spacious, courteous, courageous Don't like—vicious, suspicious, contagious, infectious, mischievous

Unit 17 Words that get mixed up

A 1. The strong wind will *affect* many villages along the coast. One *effect* … 2. The teacher will not *accept* late homework, *except* ... 3. If you want to see the cassowary, stand *quite* still and be very *quiet*. 4. You should take *off* your football boots when you come in the door *of* ... 5. The button on your shirt is too *loose* and it will fall off. You will *lose* ... 6. When I was asked to *choose* a new dress, I *chose* ... 7. My friend *bought* me an ice cream. It was a hot day and by the time she/*brought* ... 8. I would like to go *to* Lae *too*, as well as Madang. 9. In the *past* we dressed in traditional costumes. Some of the traditions have been *passed* ... 10. Today is *their* holiday, so *they're* ... 11. That's my dog. The car hit *its* leg. *It's* been hurt. 12. It's *your* turn next. Are you sure *you're* ... 13. I go to basketball *practice* two days a week. At home I also *practise* ... 14. My teacher wanted to *advise* me to work harder because my marks were not good. Her *advice* ... 15. The day began with thunder and *lightning*. After the storm passed, we saw that the sky was *lightening* ...

Unit 18 Word groups—happy words

A 1. glad, 2. cheerful, 3. miracle, 4. laugh, 5. excitement, 6. sincere, 7. patient, 8. favourite, 9. courtesy, 10. loveliest

B lucky—fortunate, having good luck, convenient—easy to use, independent—not having to depend on something, pleased—happy and satisfied, easier—less difficult, familiar—something well known to you, favourite—the one you like best, cheerful—a feeling of happiness, joyful—full of joy, loveliest—the most lovely, successful—doing very well at something, excellent—the very best of something

Unit 19 Word groups—words about our world

A country—nation, altitude—height, equator—line on map, continent—large area of land, tropical—hot, climate—weather, drought—desert, monsoon—flood, latitude—location, ocean—Pacific

B 1. earth 2. equator 3. latitude and longitude 4. continents 5. islands 6. altitude 7. Desert 8. drought 9. monsoon 10. population 11. country 12. climate

C camels—desert, rainforest—tropics, heavy rain—monsoon, whales and dolphins—ocean, coconuts and reefs—island, Asia—continent

Unit 20 Word groups—words about time

A 1. century 2. daily 3. earlier 4. future 5. year

B 1. decade 2. fortnight 3. present 4. annual 5. century
6. generations 7. yesterday 8. calendar 9. weekend 10. memory

Unit 21 Word groups—words about agriculture

A 1. When you export a crop you send it out of the country.
2. When you cultivate the soil you turn it over and make it
ready for the new plants. 3. When you make compost you
put food scraps and weeds back into the soil. 4. When you
plough you use a tractor. 5. When you weed your garden
you get rid of the unwanted plants. 6. When you prune a
tree you cut off the unwanted branches. 7. When you irrigate
the land you put water on it. 8. When you manure a crop
you put animal waste on it.

B coconut palm, rubber plantation, cash crop, irrigation
pump, coffee berries, tea leaf, cocoa pod

C 1. plant 2. irrigate 3. manure 4. livestock 5. market
6. Transport 7. pruned 8. subsistence

Unit 22 Words groups—what's your job?

A 1. burglar 2. technician 3. interpreter 4. secretary
5. councillor 6. engineer 7. librarian 8. mechanic
9. storekeeper 10. wholesaler 11. scientist 12. journalist
13 reporter 14. referee 15. lawyer

B 1. referee 2. driver 3. carpenter 4. nurse, 5. storekeeper
6. scientist

C 1. storekeeper 2. pilot 3. interpreter 4. burglar 5. librarian
6. councillor

Unit 23 Word groups—words about cooking

A INGREDIENTS, Grate, tomatoes, moderate, mackerel,
ingredients, quarters, mixture, squeeze, juice, refrigerate,
taste

B 1. ingredients 2. temperature 3. refrigerate 4. simmer 5. boil
6. crumbs 7. thicken 8. peel

C 1. peel 2. mix 3. boil 4. taste 5. squeeze 6. grate 7. refrigerate
8. thicken

Unit 24 Word groups—words about music

A 1. rhythm 2. rhyme 3. voice, stage 4. notes, melody, tune
5. harmony, discord

B 1. melodious 2. rhythmic 3. tuneful 4. tuneless
5. harmonious 6. discordant 7. rhyming

C 1. rhythms, rhymes, pianos, concerts, radios, audiences,
guitars, flutes, cassettes, trumpets, discords, voices 2. basses
3. melodies, harmonies

D concert, guitars, bass, drums, trumpet, flute, piano, cassette,
tunes, radio, audience, concerts, cassette

Unit 25 Word groups—words about sports and games

B 1. late entry 2. popular hero 3. noisy spectators
4. soccer draw 5. well-kept arena

C boundary, team, challenge, referee, champion, association

D 1. The journalist wrote about the soccer game. 2. The new
team challenged the champions. 3. The spectators cheered
their team loudly. 4. The referee called for a time out. 5. Gia
was a contestant in the 500 metres race. 6. We sent a strong
team of runners to the athletics competition. 7. It is
unsporting to complain about losing the game. 8. The
contestants did not agree with the referee's decision 9. The
team was unhappy because the final score was a draw.
10. Our entry was late so we missed the competition.

Unit 26 Word groups—words about cars

A 1. license 2. drivers test 3. road rules 4. registration
5. windscreen 6. safety-sticker 7. brakes and steering
8. wipers 9. automatic, manual 10. spare, tyre, puncture

B 1. A vehicle is another name for a car, truck or PMV.
2. PMVs are very busy in Port Moresby. 3. If you buy a
second-hand car you should get the steering and brakes
checked by a mechanic. 4. Driving without a license will get
you into trouble. 5.The highway from Lae to the Highlands
is called Route 100. 6. A second-hand car is cheaper to buy
than a new one. 7. You need four-wheel drive to drive on a
muddy road. 8. If the windshield is cracked it is hard for the

driver to see the road. 9. You need to use a spare tyre when you have a puncture. 10. The road rules tell you how you must drive on the road.

Unit 27 Word groups—words about travelling

A 1. booking—reservation 2. timetable—schedule
3. bag—suitcase 4. passport and visa—papers 5. label—tag
6. trip—journey

B 1. **d**estination 2. **t**ourism 3. **d**eparture 4. **c**abin 5. **s**eatbelt
6. **a**irport 7. **l**ifeboat 8. **d**ocuments 9. **t**icket 10. **b**ag

C 2. to depart 3. to tour 4. to book

D trip, timetable, booking, tickets, papers, passport, visa,
Tourism, airport, counter, tickets, bag, label, seatbelt,
destination

Unit 28 Word groups—words about thoughts

A 1. forgive 2. enjoy 3. argue 4. worry 5. astonish 6. condemn
7. worship 8. debate

B 1. **c**hoose 2. **w**orry 3. **h**ope 4. **c**ondemn 5. **a**stonish
6. **a**pologise 7. **g**uess 8. **h**ate 9. **f**orgive 10. **b**elieve 11. **f**orget
12. **a**ccept 13. **a**gree 14. **d**reamt 15. **w**orship 16. **e**njoy
17. **a**rgue 18. **d**ebate**d** 19. **d**oubt 20. **w**ish

C hate—hatred, forgive—forgiveness, doubt—doubt,
astonish—astonishment, accept—acceptance, argue—
argument, agree—agreement, choose—choice, apologise—
apology, enjoy—enjoyment, believe—belief

Unit 29 Word groups—words about our senses

A sandpaper—rough, limestone rocks—sharp, pigs' skins—
prickly, a light wind—gentle, patting a cat—smooth,
baby's bath water—tepid

B the whistle at half-time—shrill, brakes that need oiling—
squeal, birdsong—tuneful, a live band—noisy,
contentment—sighing, a crying child——wailing

C myself in a trick mirror—distorted, a bird of paradise—
colourful, a secret cave—dark, the view from a fast moving
car—blurred, an enormous snake—scary, a bright hibiscus
flower—beautiful

D something rotten—putrid, a garden—floral, perfume—pleasant, closed up room—musty, roasting coffee—aromatic, ginger—spicy

E sugar—sweet, a green mango—sour, sea water—salty, quinine medicine—bitter, a juicy pawpaw—succulent, a meat pie—savoury

F 1. smooth—rough 2. blurred—clear 3. salty—sugary
4. tepid—boiling 5. bitter—sweet 6. sharp—blunt
7. shrill——tuneful
1. noisy—quiet 2. beautiful—ugly 3. prickly—smooth
4. sour—sweet 5. dark—light 6. colourful—colourless
7. musty—fresh

Unit 30 Word groups—words about culture

A Per<u>dance</u>st, of<u>feather</u>st, inter<u>family</u>ald, con<u>sago</u>se, per<u>funeral</u>ise, super<u>custom</u>ite, bi<u>legend</u>court, mal<u>feast</u>age, combo<u>culture</u>ate

C 1. Our family makes clay pots and trades them. 2. Our clan has a legend about how the bird of paradise got its colours. 3. We exchange special bananas for bride price. 4. We live with our aunt, uncles and other members of our extended family. 5. The lakatoi was used for the Hiri trade. 6. In Milne Bay shells are traded in the Kula ring. 7. Many things such as language and customs make up a clan's culture. 8. We have a feast for a dead person one year after they die. 9. Our clan cries for many days when there is a funeral. 10. The conch shell was used to call members of the clan to come and meet. 11. A pig exchange means many pigs are killed. 12. Many headdresses that are used for dances are made from feathers. 13. We help keep our tradition when we teach the children our language. 14. Sago was traditionally traded for clay pots. 15. The kina shell was traded into the Highlands, and used for wearing. 16. We learn about culture from our extended families.

Unit 31 Word groups—words about business

A calcu/lator, che/que, acc/ounts, whole/sale, ret/ail, let/ter, ex/port

B 1. export 2. import 3. buy 4. sell 5. transport 6. profit
7. loss 8. cheque 9. account book 10. envelop

C 1. An office is where the businessman does his business.
2. Money collected from taxes is used by the government.
3. A retailer gets store goods from a wholesale store.
4. The retail store sells to the customer. 5. A profit is when
you make more money than your costs. 6. You need to open
a bank account for your business. 7. Some businesses need a
bank loan to start their business. 8. You need to write your
profit and costs in an account book. 9. A calculator will help
you keep your accounts. 10. A loss is when you do not make
a profit.

Unit 32 Word groups—words about medicine

A 1. malaria 2. diarrhoea 3. patient 4. emergency
5. ambulance 6. medicine 7. hospital 8. injection
9. infectious 10. bandage

B 1. Pneumonia 2. bandage 3. preventible 4. Acquired
Immune Deficiency Disease 5. hospital 6. clinic
7. infectious 8. Typhoid 9. ulcer 10. Malnutrition

Unit 33 Word groups—words to use for discussing ideas

A 1. argue 2. opposed to 3. conclusion 4. introduction
5. summary 6. opponent 7. opinion 8. facts 9. speaker
10. arguing

B argue—argument, plan—plan, think—thought,
support—support, agree—agreement

C 1. argument 2. introduction 3. summary 4. arguing facts
5. opponent 6. support 7. side, plan 8. agree

Unit 34 Word groups—words to use when applying for a job

A 1. application 2. reference 3. photocopy 4. headmaster
5. interview 6. advertised 7. certificate 8. punctual
9. position 10. experience

B apply, clerk, advertised, finished, enclose, photocopy, certificate, results, experience, supervisor, reference, reference, headmaster, interview

C 1. school—headmaster 2. enclose—inside
3. photocopy—machine 4. results—marks
5. on time—punctual
1. finished—completed 2. supervisor—boss
3. advertised—newspaper 4. position—job
5. application—apply